Super Sound

Wendy Madgwick

WAYLAND

Titles in this series:
Up in the Air • Water Play • Magnets and Sparks • Super Sound
Super Materials • Light and Dark • Living Things • On the Move

First published in 1998 by Wayland (Publishers) Ltd,
61 Western Road, Hove, East Sussex BN3 1JD, England.

Series devised by Tucker Slingsby Ltd, Berkeley House,
73 Upper Richmond Road, London SW15 2SZ

Designer: Anita Ruddell
Illustrations: Catherine Ward/Simon Girling Associates
Photographer: Andrew Sydenham

Many thanks to Aneesah, Ben, Claire, Kieran, Luke, May,
Poppy and William

Picture Acknowledgements: pages 5, 6 top, 6 bottom, 13, 16
Zefa; page 21 Trip.

Words that appear in **bold** in the text are explained in the glossary on page 30.

British Library Cataloguing in Publication Data
Madgwick, Wendy
Super Sound. - (Science Starters)
I. Sound. - Juvenile literature
I. Title II. Ward, Catherine
534
ISBN 0 7502 2161 5

Colour reproduction by Page Turn, Hove
Printed and bound by G. Canale & C.S.p.A., Turin

Contents

Looking at sound

This book has lots of fun activities to help you find out about sound. Here are some simple rules you should follow before doing an activity.

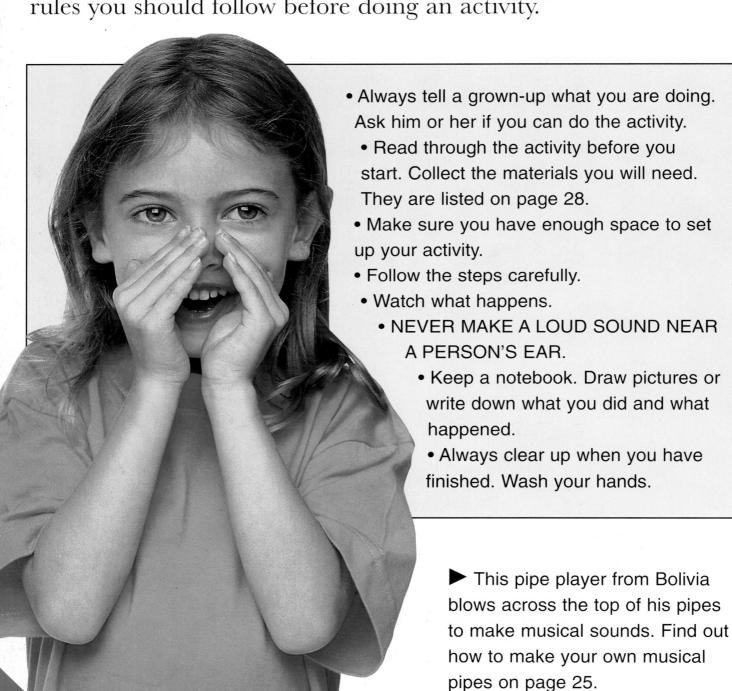

- Always tell a grown-up what you are doing. Ask him or her if you can do the activity.
- Read through the activity before you start. Collect the materials you will need. They are listed on page 28.
- Make sure you have enough space to set up your activity.
- Follow the steps carefully.
- Watch what happens.
- NEVER MAKE A LOUD SOUND NEAR A PERSON'S EAR.
- Keep a notebook. Draw pictures or write down what you did and what happened.
- Always clear up when you have finished. Wash your hands.

► This pipe player from Bolivia blows across the top of his pipes to make musical sounds. Find out how to make your own musical pipes on page 25.

Noisy noise

Noise is all around us. You cannot see noise, but you can hear it. Listen hard. How many different noises can you hear?

Having fun

Is this swimming pool a noisy place?
What sounds would you hear if you were there?
What sounds would be loud?
What sounds would be soft?

Peace and quiet

Is this river bank a noisier place or a quieter place than the swimming pool?
What sounds would you hear?

The crowded swimming pool would be noisier than the peaceful river bank. But there would be lots of different sounds in both places.

Sound shapes

How do you make different sounds?
Let's find out.

1 Make an 'oh' sound. What shape do your lips make? Where is your tongue?

2 Make an 'ah' sound. What shape do your lips make now? Where is your tongue now?

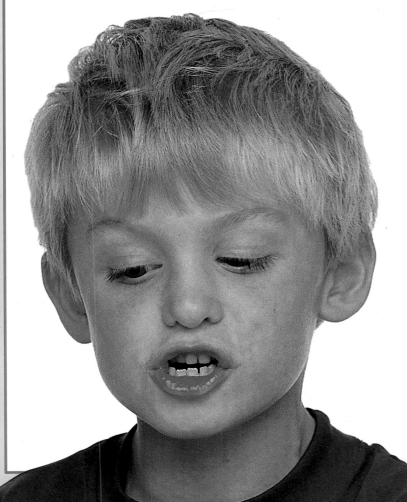

3 Make 'ee', 'ss', 'tee', 'pee' and 'bee' sounds. How do your lips change shape? Do you put your tongue in different places?

◄ This boy is talking. He is using his lips and tongue to make different sounds.

7

Travelling sounds

Different materials make different sounds. Sounds travel to your ears through the air. Sound can also travel through other materials.

Make as many sounds as you can using materials like those shown above. Listen to the different sounds.

Plastic cup telephones

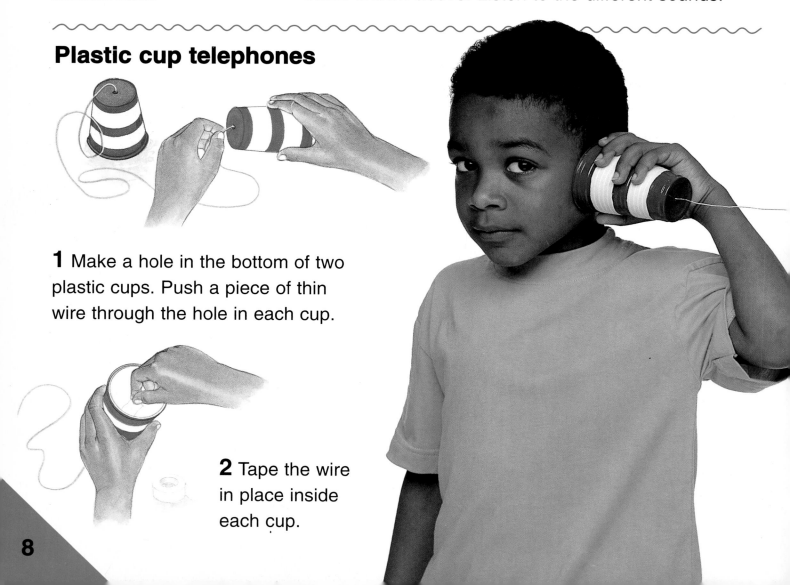

1 Make a hole in the bottom of two plastic cups. Push a piece of thin wire through the hole in each cup.

2 Tape the wire in place inside each cup.

8

Sending sounds

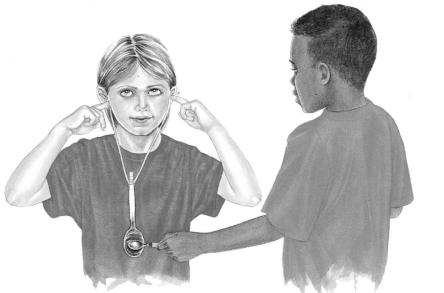

1 Tape two pieces of thick string to a spoon. Hold the spoon up by the strings. Ask a friend to tap the spoon with another spoon. Can you hear the sound?

2 Put the strings flat against your ears. Ask your friend to tap the spoon again. The sound is louder. You can hear the sound through the strings. The strings **transmit** sound.

3 Give one cup to a friend. Keep the other cup. Move apart so that the wire is pulled tight. Turn away from your friend. Put your plastic cup to your ear. Ask your friend to whisper a message into his or her cup. Can you hear the message?

Take care with these experiments. Do not push anything into your ears.

Feeling sounds

When something makes a sound it moves
backwards and forwards very quickly.
We call these movements **vibrations**.
We can feel these vibrations.

Moving throats

Put your fingers lightly on the front of
your throat. Keep quiet. Can you feel
your throat moving? Say something.
Can you feel your throat moving?
These movements are sound vibrations
made when you talk.

Wobbling lips

Rest your fingers lightly on your
lips. What can you feel?
Make a loud 'ooh' sound.
What can you feel?
You should be able to feel
your lips **vibrating**.

Vibrating balloons

You can feel the sounds made by a radio.

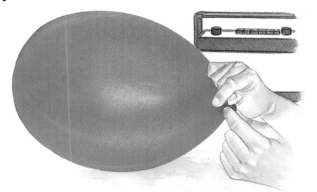

1 Blow up a balloon and knot the end. Turn the radio off. Hold the balloon between your hands. Put it against the front of the radio's loudspeaker. What can you feel? The balloon should not move.

2 Turn on the radio. Hold the balloon against the radio's loudspeaker. What can you feel? You should feel the balloon vibrating.

3 Try loud music and quiet music. Do the vibrations of the balloon feel different? The vibrations should be biggest when the music is loudest.

'Seeing' sound

When an object vibrates, it makes the air around it vibrate. The air carries these vibrations to your ears. You hear the sound. We can 'see' sound using these vibrations.

Bouncing balls

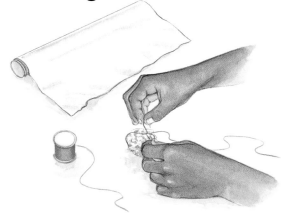

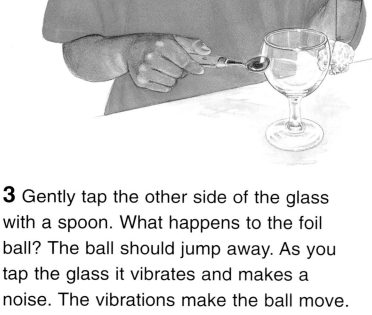

1 Screw up some kitchen foil into a ball. Tie a piece of thread round the foil.

2 Put a wine glass on a table. Hold the thread so that the foil ball just touches the glass.

3 Gently tap the other side of the glass with a spoon. What happens to the foil ball? The ball should jump away. As you tap the glass it vibrates and makes a noise. The vibrations make the ball move.

▶ This machine shows sounds as pictures on a screen. The jagged lines indicate a loud sound.

Jumping salt

1 Stretch cling film over the open top of a large metal can. Keep it in place with a rubber band. Sprinkle salt on top of the cling film.

2 Hold a large tin tray close to the can and hit it hard with a wooden spoon. What happens to the salt? The salt jumps. This is caused by the sound vibrations made when you bang the tray.

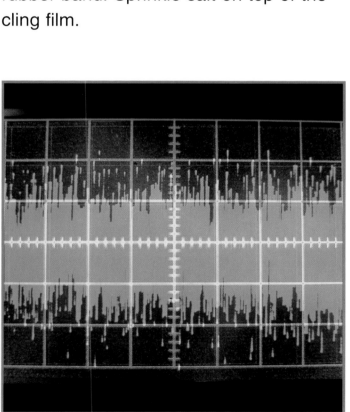

3 Hit the tray again. Put your hand against the tray to stop it moving. What happens to the salt? The salt stops moving when you stop the tray vibrating.

Loud and quiet

Some sounds are loud. Some are quiet. The loudness of sounds is measured in **decibels**. A quiet whisper is about 20 decibels. The noise a jet aircraft makes is about 120 decibels.

This girl is banging a drum. The boy is cutting up paper. Which child is making the louder noise?

What is the loudest noise you have ever heard? What quiet sounds have you heard?

Snap bang!

Make a noisy paper clacker.

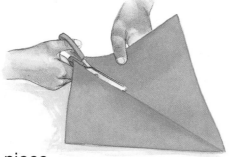

1 Fold a piece of paper, 20 cm square, in half to make a triangle. Cut along the fold.

2 Draw lines 2 cm in from the edges of the triangle. Cut off the points as shown. Fold the paper triangle in two.

3 Fold back the side strips along the lines you drew.

4 Fold a piece of card, 20 cm square, to make a triangle. Open up the card.

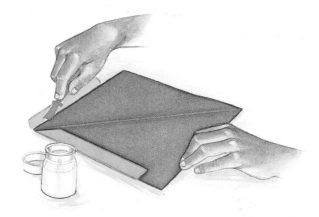

5 Place the paper triangle inside the card. Glue the side strips of the paper to the outside of the card. Let the glue dry.

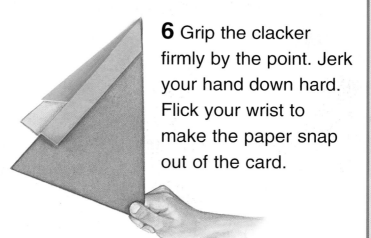

6 Grip the clacker firmly by the point. Jerk your hand down hard. Flick your wrist to make the paper snap out of the card.

Hear, hear

People hear sounds with their ears. How well can you hear? Are two ears better than one? Let's find out.

▲ The barn owl has very good hearing. It can swoop down and pick up a rustling mouse, even in the dark.

Super ears

Ask some friends to help. Blindfold your friends and position them about 1 m away, with their backs to you.

Drop a button on to the floor. Ask each child who hears the sound to take a step forward.

Keep dropping the button until no one hears it fall. How far away can your friends hear the button fall?

'Ear, 'ear!

1 Ask a friend to blindfold you. Your friend should hold a ticking clock and stand in different places. Can you tell where the ticking is coming from?

3 Now try it with your right ear covered.

It should be much easier to guess the position of the clock using two ears.

2 Cover your left ear so that you cannot hear with it. Is it harder to tell where the clock is?

What's that?

If you trap sounds they seem louder. Sounds bounce back off some objects making **echoes**.

Ear trumpet or megaphone?

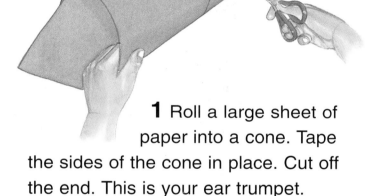

1 Roll a large sheet of paper into a cone. Tape the sides of the cone in place. Cut off the end. This is your ear trumpet.

3 Listen to your friend shout with and without a megaphone. Your friend's voice should sound louder with a megaphone.

2 Make another cone. Give one to a friend. Ask the friend to shout into the narrow end to make a megaphone.

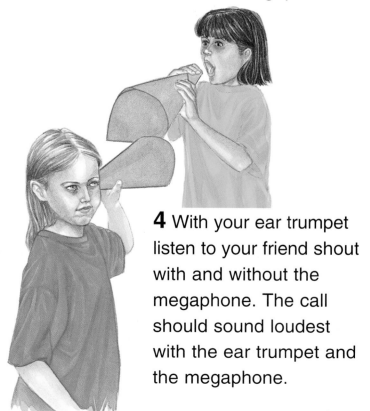

4 With your ear trumpet listen to your friend shout with and without the megaphone. The call should sound loudest with the ear trumpet and the megaphone.

Bouncing sounds

1 Shout out loud. Then shout into an empty bucket. Does your voice sound louder? Your voice echoes in the empty bucket.

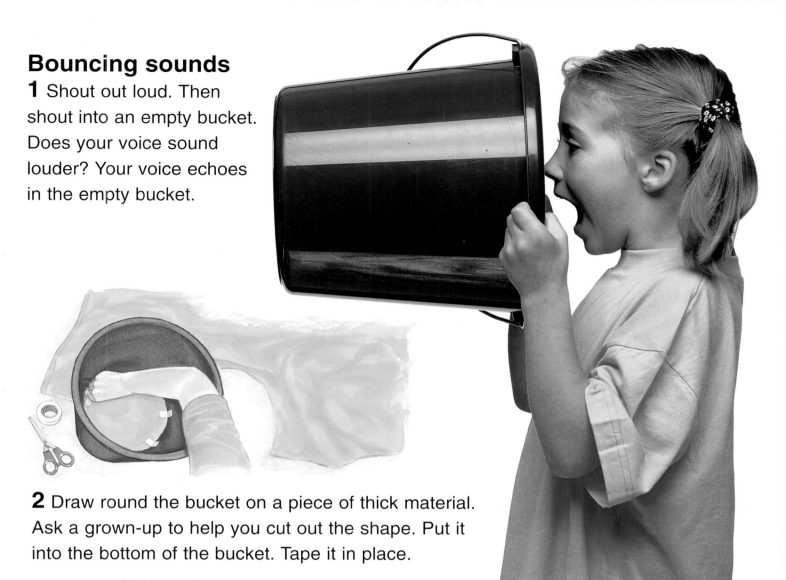

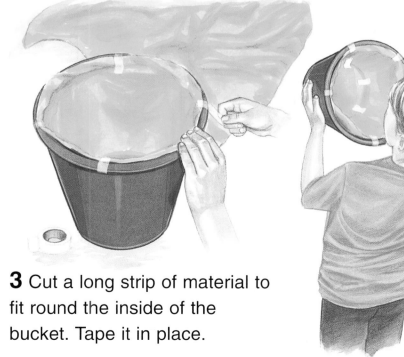

2 Draw round the bucket on a piece of thick material. Ask a grown-up to help you cut out the shape. Put it into the bottom of the bucket. Tape it in place.

3 Cut a long strip of material to fit round the inside of the bucket. Tape it in place.

4 Shout into the bucket. Listen to the echo. The material soaks up the sound. The echo is quieter when you shout into the lined bucket.

Peace and quiet

If sounds are very loud, they can hurt your ears.
People in noisy jobs wear ear protectors
to muffle sound and protect their ears
from the noise.

Ear protectors

1 Ask a friend to drop a marble into a tin. Listen to the noise it makes.

3 To make your own ear protectors, fill both tubs with cotton wool. Hold them over your ears. Try the marble test again. Is the sound as loud?

Fill your ear protectors with different materials. Try tissue paper, kitchen foil, paper and wool. Which fillings keep the sound out best?

2 Hold the empty tubs over your ears. Ask your friend to drop the marble from the same height. Is the sound as loud?

► This man is using a very noisy drill. Can you see his ear protectors? These help to stop the noise reaching his ears.

Shake and chime

Some musical **instruments** make a sound when they are hit. They are called **percussion** instruments. Let's make some.

Shaking sounds

1 Decorate two plastic bottles. Put small pebbles in one bottle and rice grains in the other. Put the lids back on. These are your shakers.

2 Shake the bottles. Do they sound different? Make shakers with as many different sounds as you can. Try making shakers filled with dried macaroni, dried beans and sugar.

Clinking chimes

1 Tie and tape pieces of string to some long, thin objects.

2 Rest a long piece of wood between two chairs. Tie the strings to the wood.

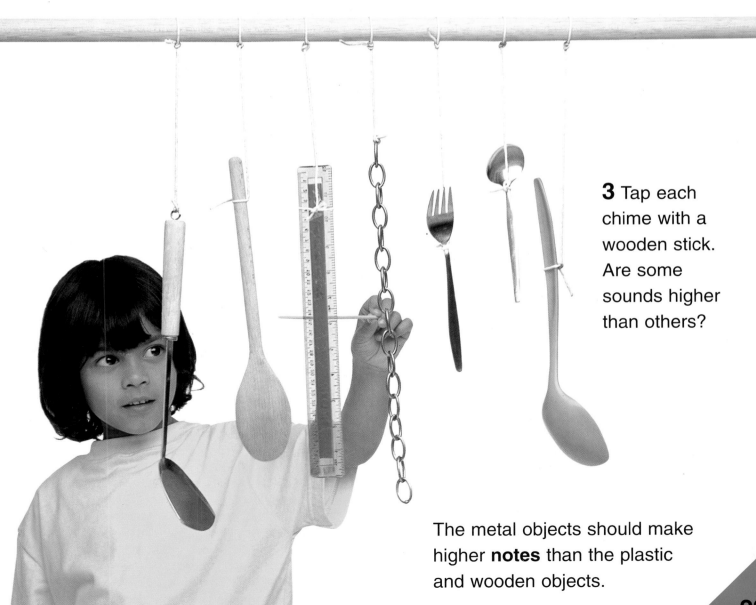

3 Tap each chime with a wooden stick. Are some sounds higher than others?

The metal objects should make higher **notes** than the plastic and wooden objects.

Bottles and pipes

A musical note can be made if you blow across the top of an empty bottle. This happens because the air in the bottle vibrates. Many wind instruments work in the same way.

Bottle pipes

1 Stand five empty plastic bottles of the same size and shape in a line.

2 Fill one bottle with a little water. Pour more water into each bottle in the line.

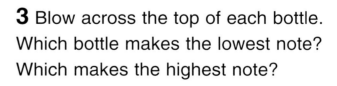

3 Blow across the top of each bottle. Which bottle makes the lowest note? Which makes the highest note?

The bottle with the most water makes the highest note. The air vibrates more slowly in the bottles with less water and more air. They make lower notes.

Pipe it

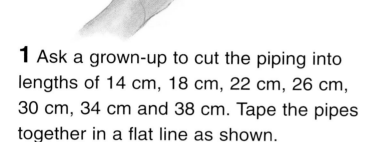

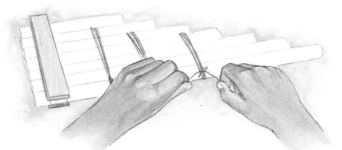

2 Glue a flat piece of wood to either side of the pipes over the tape. Tie the pipes together.

1 Ask a grown-up to cut the piping into lengths of 14 cm, 18 cm, 22 cm, 26 cm, 30 cm, 34 cm and 38 cm. Tape the pipes together in a flat line as shown.

3 Blow across the top of the pipes to make different sounds. The longest pipe with the most air in it makes the lowest note. The shortest pipe with the least air makes the highest note.

◄ This girl is playing a recorder. She blows into it to make the air vibrate. She changes the notes by putting her fingers over the holes.

String along

Musical sounds can be made by vibrating strings. This is how stringed instruments work.

Box guitar

1 Cut a hole near one end of the lid of a plastic or cardboard box. Stick a thin piece of wood or cork across the box above the hole. Decorate your guitar.

2 Stretch the elastic bands round the box. Put thicker bands near one side and thinner bands near the other.

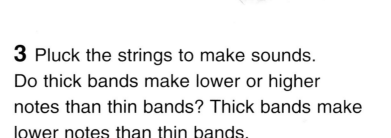

3 Pluck the strings to make sounds. Do thick bands make lower or higher notes than thin bands? Thick bands make lower notes than thin bands.

Stringed card

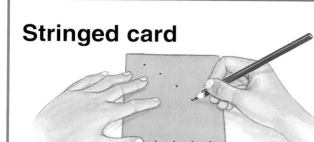

1 Cut a piece of thick card 14 cm wide and 12 cm long. Draw two rows of dots as shown.

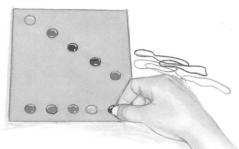

2 Press a drawing pin into each dot. Stretch a small elastic band of the same size round each pair of drawing pins.

3 Pluck the bands with your fingers. Which band makes the highest sound?
The band that is stretched the most makes the highest note.

◀ This boy is playing a violin. The bow makes the strings vibrate. Notes are made by pressing down on the strings with the fingers.

Materials you will need

p. 6 Noisy noise - mirror.

p. 8 Travelling sounds - kitchen foil, paper, metal can, small stones, empty plastic bottle, scrubbing brush, metal spoon, string, round-ended scissors, two plastic cups, thin wire, sticky tape, a drawing pin to make a hole in the bottom of each plastic cup. Ask a friend to help.

p. 10 Feeling sounds - radio, balloon.

p. 12 'Seeing' sound - kitchen foil, thread, sticky tape, wine glass, spoon, cling film, metal can, elastic band, salt, tin tray, wooden spoon.

p. 14 Loud and quiet - pencil, ruler, 20 cm square piece of paper, 20 cm square card, round-ended scissors, glue.

p. 16 Hear, hear - button, ticking clock, two scarves. Ask two friends to join in.

p. 18 What's that? - two large sheets of paper, sticky tape, round-ended scissors, empty bucket, large piece of thick material, washable felt-tipped pen. Ask a grown-up to help you.

p. 20 Peace and quiet - two plastic food tubs, marble, metal can, cotton wool, tissue paper, kitchen foil, paper, wool. Ask a friend to help you.

p. 22 Shake and chime - two plastic bottles, small pebbles, dried macaroni, dried beans, rice, sugar, colourful stickers, metal cutlery, plastic ruler, wooden spoon, long piece of wood (a broom handle would be good), string, sticky tape, wooden stick.

p. 24 Bottles and pipes - five empty plastic bottles of the same size and shape, water, 2 m of 2 cm diameter plastic plumbers' piping, sticky tape, two flat pieces of wood 15 cm by 2 cm. Ask a grown-up to cut the piping.

p. 26 String along - five elastic bands of the same size ranging from thick to thin, five small elastic bands, plastic or cardboard box, pencil, ruler, thick card, 10 drawing pins.

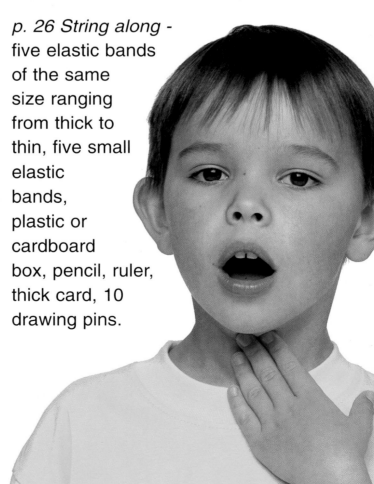

Hints to helpers

Pages 6 and 7

Discuss different kinds of loud and soft noises. Compare the different sounds you would hear in a swimming pool, eg children shouting, water splashing etc, and by a river bank, eg birds singing, rippling water etc.

Discuss why it is so important to move your lips and tongue properly when speaking. This helps you make clear sounds.

Pages 8 and 9

Discuss the sounds made by different materials. Discuss how sounds travel through the air. Air particles are pushed together by the sound vibrations. These pushing movements cause a sound wave to form which spreads out through the air in all directions. It is rather like the ripple that forms when you drop a pebble into a pool of water.

Particles in solids are closer together than in air, so the sound waves travel better and faster through solids.

Some materials transmit the sounds better than others. They are good sound conductors. Test different materials to find out how well they transmit sound. Tape the spoon to strips of wood, plastic and thin wire. The thin wire and string should transmit the sounds better than plastic and wood.

Pages 10 and 11

Discuss how we make sounds when we talk. At the top of the wind pipe are two vocal cords. These are tiny bands of tissue that vibrate as air passes through them. As they vibrate they make a sound.

Discuss how we hear sounds. When something moves quickly or vibrates it makes a sound wave that travels through the air. The louder the noise the larger the vibration and sound wave. The lower the noise, the further apart the vibrations and the further apart the waves. With high notes the vibrations are very close together, so the individual waves are close together.

Pages 12 and 13

When the glass is tapped, it vibrates and sends sound waves through the air. When the sound waves hit the foil ball, the foil ball also vibrates and moves away from the glass.

When the tray is hit it shakes and makes a sound. The sound waves travel through the air and hit the cling film covering the tin. The cling film vibrates and makes the salt jump. Explain how a similar thing occurs in the ear when we hear. Sound waves make the skin of the eardrum vibrate. This sends messages to the brain about the sounds so that we can 'hear' them.

Touching the tray stops it vibrating and so the sound stops too. The sound waves no longer hit the cling film so the salt stops moving.

Page 15

Try to find out what makes the loudest clacker. Make bigger and smaller clackers with thicker and thinner cards and paper for the middle. Try smaller and larger pieces of paper for the middle section and see which makes the loudest bang. The larger clackers and the clackers with the largest piece of paper in the centre should make the loudest bang.

Page 17

Explain that we can tell the direction of a sound because we have two ears. Each ear receives the sound at a slightly different time, so our brain can work out the direction the sound is coming from.

Pages 18 and 19

Discuss how it is easier to hear sounds if we concentrate the sound waves and channel them into our ears. Our outer ears do this to some extent. Some animals that depend on hearing rather than sight have large outer ears to catch the slightest sound and channel it into the ear. A megaphone also channels sound. It directs the sound in one direction instead of letting it spread out.

Discuss how hard surfaces reflect sound. Sound can be reflected in the same way as light. We hear the reflected sound as an echo. Soft surfaces absorb the sounds, so you do not hear an echo.

Page 21

As with the test on page 19, the softer materials should absorb the sound more than the hard materials. The cotton wool should make the best ear protectors.

Page 23

When you hit the metal objects they vibrate more quickly than the plastic or wooden objects. This means that the individual waves of the sound waves are closer together, so they produce higher sounds or notes.

Pages 24 and 25

The bottle pipe with the most water has only a short column of air. As you blow across the top, the air in the bottle vibrates. The vibrations travel quickly up and down the short column of air making a high note. In the bottles with only a small amount of water, there is a long column of air. The vibrations travel more slowly so the note is lower.

The pan pipes work in a similar way. The longer pipes with the most air vibrate more slowly and so make lower notes.

A small set of pipes can be made using drinking straws if plumbers' piping is not available.

Pages 26 and 27

Discuss how the piece of cork or wood across the box guitar acts like a bridge on a proper guitar to lift the elastic bands so that they can vibrate easily. The thicker bands vibrate more slowly than the thinner bands so they make lower notes. The vibrating elastic bands make the air in and around the box guitar vibrate. The box acts as a sound box and makes the sound waves louder — it amplifies them. Therefore the box guitar makes a louder sound than the stringed card.

The stretched bands on the stringed card vibrate quickly, so they make high notes. The looser, less stretched bands vibrate more slowly and make lower notes.

Glossary

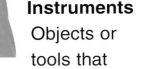

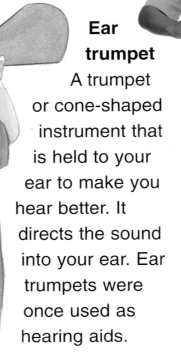

Decibels Units for measuring the loudness of a sound. Soft sounds only measure a few decibels. Loud sounds measure a large number of decibels. People need to measure the amount of noise being made, especially where there are noisy machines. Some loud noises measuring a high number of decibels can hurt your ears.

Ear trumpet A trumpet or cone-shaped instrument that is held to your ear to make you hear better. It directs the sound into your ear. Ear trumpets were once used as hearing aids.

Echoes When sounds hit a solid object they bounce back. We say they are reflected. The sounds that bounce back into your ears are called echoes.

Instruments Objects or tools that can be used to do a special job. Musical instruments are used to make music.

Megaphone A funnel or cone-shaped instrument that makes your voice sound louder.

Note A musical sound. A song or piece of music is made up of many different notes played in a particular order.

Percussion Musical instruments that make a sound when they are struck with sticks or hammers.

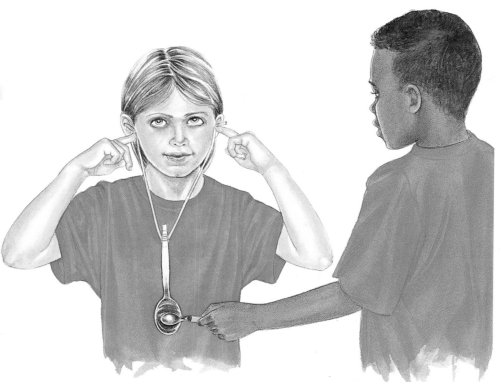

Transmit To transfer or pass. To allow sounds to pass from one place or person to another.

Vibrating When something moves up and down, or backwards and forwards, very quickly.

Vibrations Fast vibrating movements. Vibrations are often too fast for you to see, but you can hear the noise they make. If you touch something that is making a noise, you may be able to feel the vibrations.

Further reading

Hearing Sounds by Gary Gibson, Science for Fun. 1994; Franklin Watts, London

Music and Sound by Mark Pettigrew, Simply Science. 1990; Franklin Watts, London.

Science Magic with Sound by Chris Oxlade, Science Magic. 1993; Franklin Watts, London

Sound by Rosie Dalzell, Bright Sparks. 1992; Cherrytree Books, Bath.

Sound by Kay Davies and Wendy Oldfield, Simple Science. 1994; Wayland, Hove.

Sound and Music by Kay Davies and Wendy Oldfield, Starting Science. 1990; Wayland, Hove.

Index